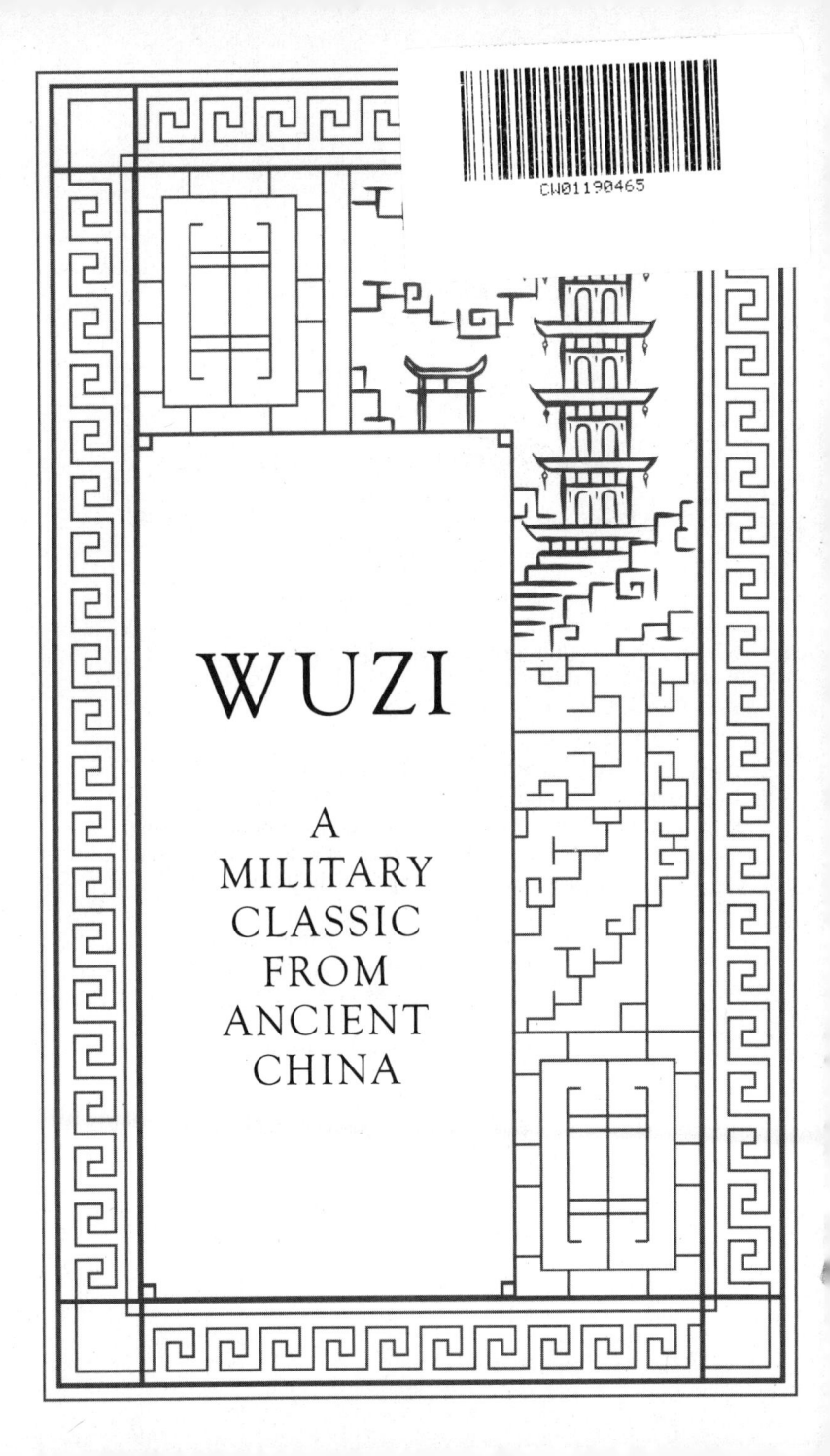

WUZI

A MILITARY CLASSIC FROM ANCIENT CHINA

Cherry Stone Publishing, an imprint of
Sweet Cherry Publishing Limited
Unit 36, Vulcan House,
Vulcan Road,
Leicester, LE5 3EF
United Kingdom

First published by Cherry Stone Publishing in 2021
2021 edition

2 4 6 8 10 9 7 5 3 1

ISBN: 978-1-78226-964-9

© Sweet Cherry Publishing

Wuzi

All rights reserved. No part of this publication may be
reproduced or utilised in any form or by any means, electronic
or mechanical, including photocopying, recording, or using
any information storage and retrieval system, without prior
permission in writing from the publisher.

This book is copyright under the Berne Convention.
No reproduction without permission.
All rights reserved.

Cover design and illustrations
by Sophie Jones

www.cherrystonepublishing.com

Printed and bound in India
I.TP002

WUZI

WU QI'S MILITARY THOUGHTS

CHERRY STONE
PUBLISHING

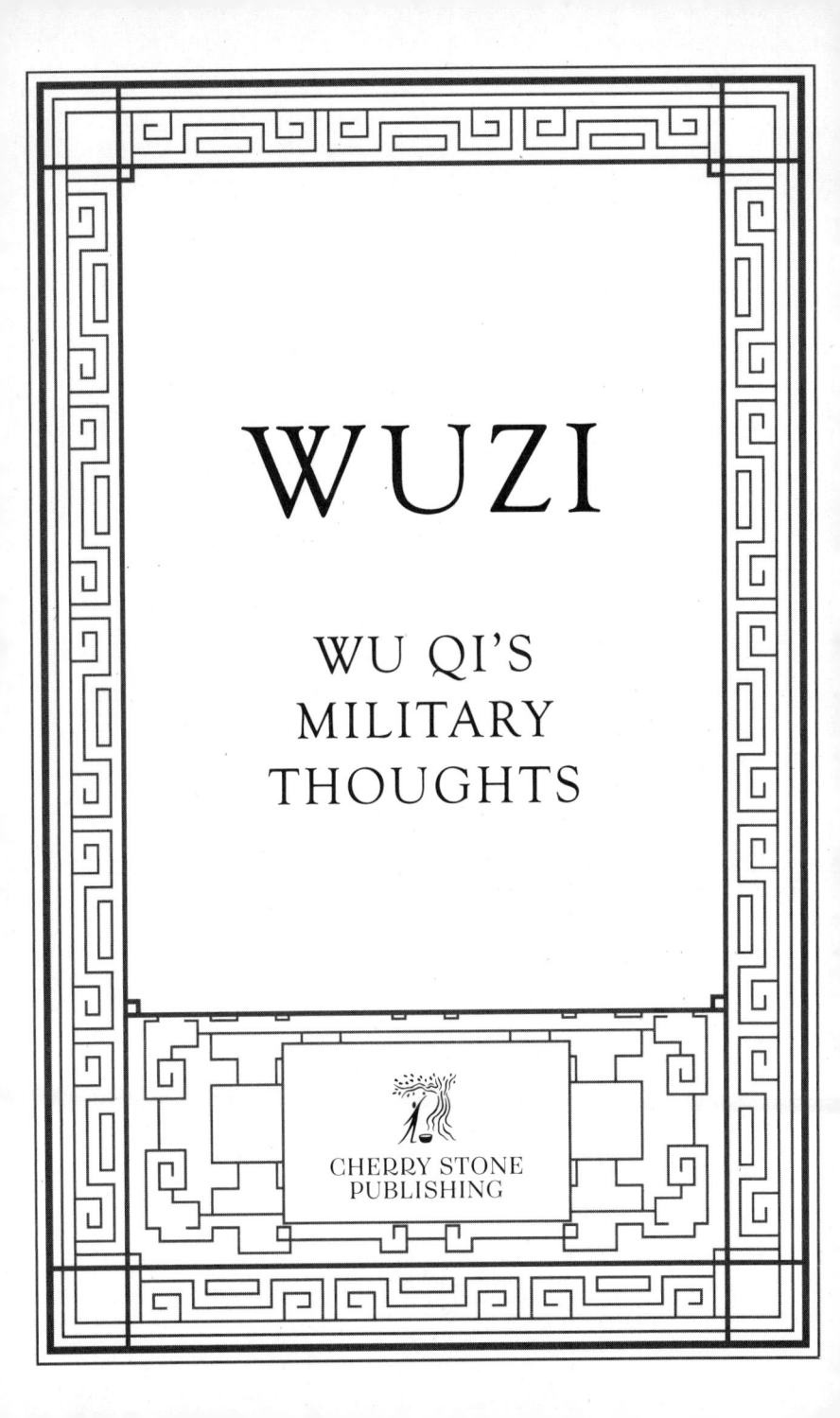

CHAPTER I.

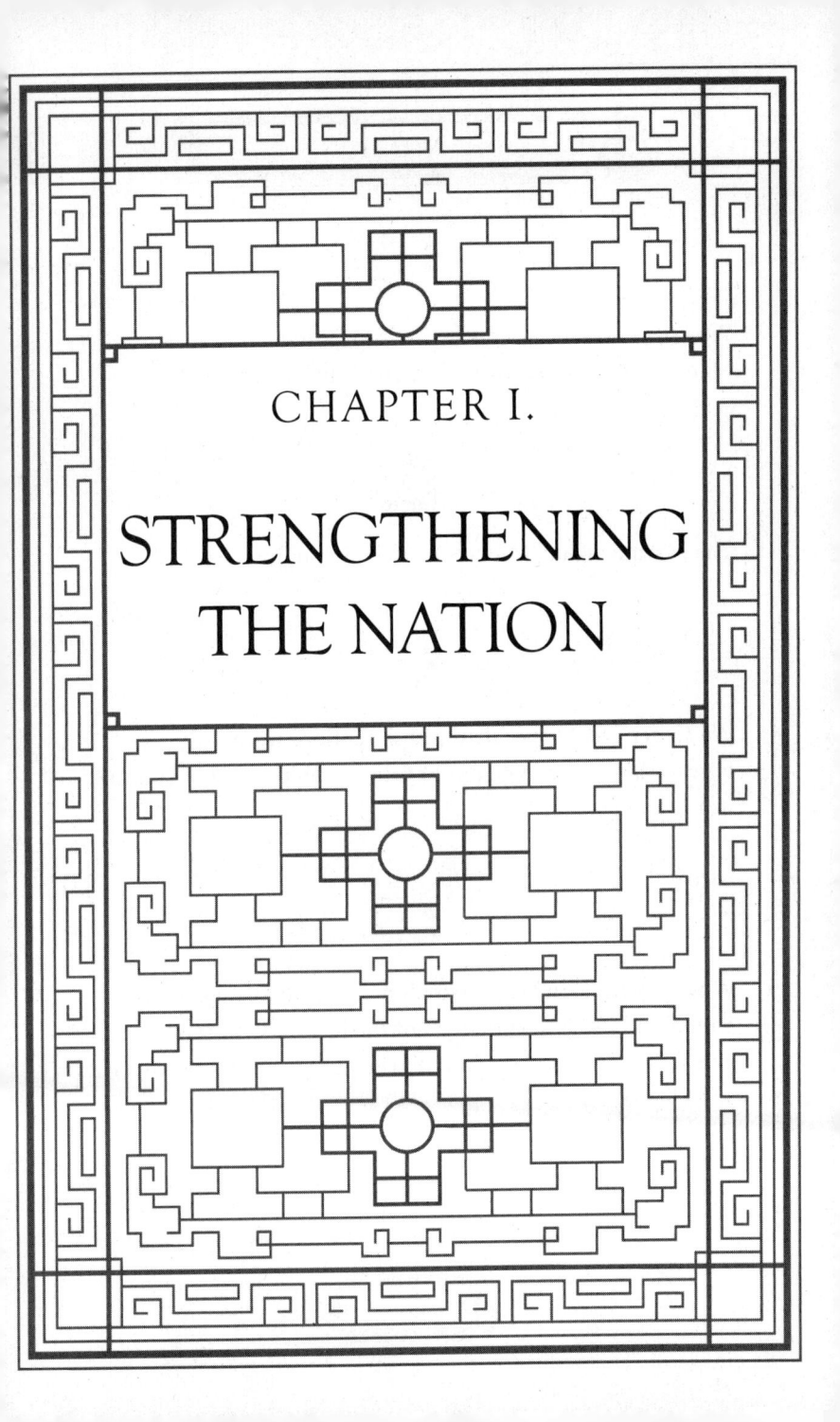

STRENGTHENING THE NATION

WUZI

1

Wu Qi, in his official Confucian dress, entered to see the Marquis Wen of Wei with his theories of warfare.

2

The Marquis said: "Military matters do not interest me."

3

Wu Qi replied: "I speculate your intentions from daily observation, and perceive your future ambitions from your past words and deeds.

4

Why do you say what you don't mean? You kill and skin animals all the year round, paint the leather with red lacquer, give it colours and then iron on the designs of rhinoceroses and elephants.

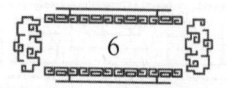

STRENGTHENING THE NATION

5

If it is used for clothing, then it is neither warm in winter nor cool in summer.

6

You have long halberds of two *zhang* and four *chi** long, and the short halberds of one *zhang* and two *chi* long.

7

The heavy chariots are covered with leather, and so are the wheels and hubs.

8

They are not magnificent to the eye; nor are they light to sit in for hunting.

---

*zhang and chi are traditional Chinese units of measurement; zhang is about 3.2m and chi is about 0.32m.

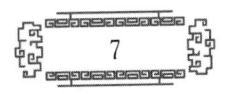

WUZI

9

So I wonder what you need these things for.

10

You claim you are going to use them in battle, but you do not seek someone who can use them.

11

This is similar to a nesting hen fighting a wild cat, or a newborn puppy going to confront a tiger.

12

For all the determination to fight, death is sure to follow.

13

In the old days, the ruler of the Chengsang Clan was a man of virtue, but not a man of arms; so he died.

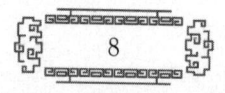

STRENGTHENING THE NATION

14

The ruler of the Youhu Clan also lost his land; although he boasted a strong army and was brave and warlike, he failed to cultivate civilization and virtue.

15

In view of this, a wise ruler must cultivate civil virtue internally and prepare for war externally.

16

Therefore, to face the enemy and not dare to enter into battle is not righteousness; to look at the bodies of fallen soldiers and grieve is not benevolence."

17

The Marquis then hosted a banquet with his wife, serving wine for Wu Qi; he invited Wu Qi to the ancestral temple and appointed him as the great general to preside over the defence of the West River.

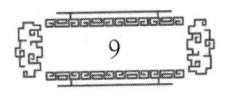

WUZI

18

Wu Qi fought seventy-six battles with various vassal states and won sixty-four times; the remaining twelve were too close to call.

19

Thanks to Wu Qi's strategies, the expansion of Wei's territory to the four sides reached up to one thousand *li**.

20

Wu Qi said: "In the old days, monarchs who sought to rule the state well must first educate the people before winning their hearts and minds.

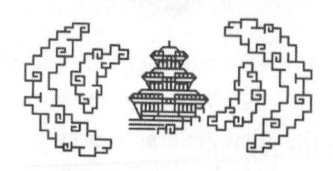

---

*li is a traditional Chinese unit of distance that is about one third of a mile.

STRENGTHENING THE NATION

21

It is not advisable to act under four kinds of incongruities: if there is no unity of will at home, no troops should be sent out; if there is no unity within the army, no battle should be fought; if the battle formation is not neat and tidy, no war should be launched; and if the actions of the soldiers are not coordinated, no victory is possible.

22

Therefore, when a wise ruler prepares to use his people to fight, he must first improve the solidarity before going to war.

23

However, he is still not fully convinced of his plans, so he goes to make sacrifices to the ancestral temples, divines the good fortune, consults the heavenly times, and obtains auspicious signs before taking action.

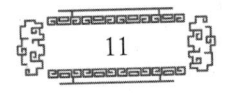

WUZI

24

Make sure the people know that the king loves their lives, laments their deaths, and that he is a considerate man.

25

Then lead the people to war so that they will feel honoured to die with their best efforts and shamed to retreat for survival."

26

Wu Qi said: "The 'way' is used to restore people's good nature.

27

'Righteousness' is used to build a career.

28

'Scheming' is used to seek profit and avoid harm.

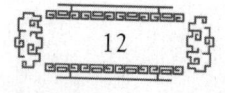

STRENGTHENING THE NATION

29

'Do' is used to consolidate and preserve the achievements of the cause.

30

If the behaviour is not in line with the 'way', and the action is not in line with the 'righteousness', then those who have power and assume important positions will cause disasters.

31

Therefore, sages use the 'way' to pacify the world, 'righteousness' to govern the state, 'propriety' to mobilise the people, and 'benevolence' to soothe the masses.

32

If these four virtues are promoted, a state will flourish; but if they are abandoned, the state will fall.

WUZI

33

That is why the people of the Xia Dynasty were happy when Shang Tang crushed Xia Jie, and the Yin people did not oppose when King Wu of Zhou crushed Yin Zhou.

34

This is because they conducted the war in accordance with the principles of heaven and the public mood."

35

Wu Qi said: "Whenever you govern a country or an army, you must educate people with rituals and encourage them with righteousness, so that they will have a sense of shame.

36

With a sense of shame, they will be able to go to war when they are strong and to defend when they are weak.

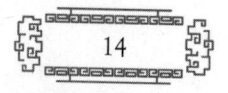

STRENGTHENING THE NATION

37

However, it is easy to achieve victory, but difficult to consolidate it.

38

Therefore, if a state engages in war, those who win five battles out of five will bring disaster (in order to preserve the results of the five victories); those who win four battles out of five will suffer from weaker national strength (in order to preserve the results of the four victories).

39

However, (thanks to the fact that less resources are spent on consolidating victories) those who win three battles will be able to dominate; those who win two battles will be able to become a king; and those who win one battle will be able to build an empire.

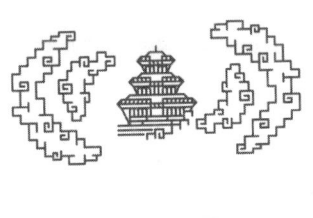

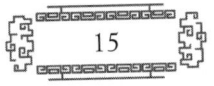

WUZI

40

Therefore, there are only few who have conquered by winning many wars, but many who have died as a result."

41

Wu Qi said: "There are five causes of war: first, the struggle for fame; second, the struggle for profit; third, the accumulation of hatred; fourth, an internal strife; fifth, a famine.

42

There are also five types of the dispatch of troops: first, a righteous dispatch; second, a strong dispatch; third, a furious dispatch; fourth, a violent dispatch; fifth, a rebellious dispatch.

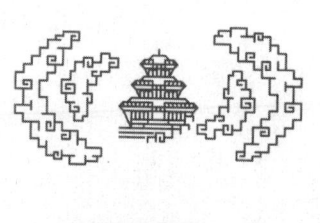

STRENGTHENING THE NATION

43

The righteous dispatch prohibits violence, eliminates chaos and saves the distress; the strong dispatch aims at conquering other states on the basis of the large number of soldiers; the furious dispatch is conducted out of anger; the violent dispatch is greedy for profits from war; and the rebellious dispatch mobilises the army despite the national chaos and fatigue.

44

To deal with these five different types of dispatch, each has a different counter-move: use reason to convince soldiers of a righteous dispatch; use humility to convince soldiers of a strong dispatch; use words to convince soldiers of a furious dispatch; use tactics to subdue soldiers of a violent dispatch; use power to contain soldiers of a rebellious dispatch."

45

Marquis Wu said to Wu Qi: "I would like to know how to govern the army, count the population, and consolidate the state."

WUZI

46

Wu Qi replied: "In ancient times, a wise ruler would strictly observe the etiquette between the ruler and his ministers as well as the law between the top and the bottom, make sure that the officials and the people were in their place, educate them according to the customs, and select competent people to prevent any misfortune.

47

Duke Huan of Qi recruited fifty thousand warriors and relied on them to dominate the vassal states.

48

Duke Wen of Jin recruited forty thousand warriors as vanguard to win over the world, and Duke Mu of Qin built up an army of thirty thousand soldiers to subdue neighbouring enemy states.

STRENGTHENING THE NATION

49

Therefore, a ruler who prepares for the future must check the population.

50

He shall put the brave and strong into a team.

51

Those who are willing to serve and show their loyalty and bravery should be grouped into a team.

52

Make a team of those who can climb high and jump far, and walk lightly and well.

WUZI

53

Make a team of those who want to serve after being dismissed from office for a crime.

54

Make a team of those who have abandoned their cities and towns and sought to clean up their act.

55

These five types of teams are the elite troops in the army.

56

If there are three thousand of such men, an attack from within can break through the enemy's siege, and an attack from outside can destroy the enemy's fief."

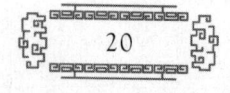

STRENGTHENING THE NATION

57

Marquis Wu said to Wu Qi: "I would like to know how to make sure that the formation is firm, the defence is solid and the battle is won."

58

Wu Qi replied: "You will see for yourself the results, instead of just knowing about them.

59

If you can employ those who have talent and virtue, but not those who don't, then the formation will be firm.

60

If the people live in peace, work happily and respect the officials, then the defence has been solidified.

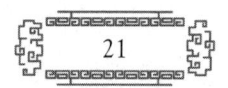

WUZI

61

When the people support their king and oppose the enemy, then the war will have been won."

62

Marquis Wu once discussed the affairs of state with his ministers, whose observations were all inferior to his. He looked delighted as he left the court.

63

Wu Qi advised him: "In the past, King Zhuang of Chu once discussed state affairs with his ministers, whose arguments were all inferior to his.

64

As he left the court, however, he looked worried.

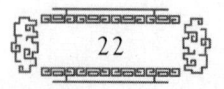

STRENGTHENING THE NATION

65

Shengong asked the king: 'Why do you look so worried?'

66

The king replied: 'I have heard that there is no shortage of sages and wise men in the state, and that those who can have them as teachers can be the king and those who can have them as friends can be hegemons.

67

Now I have no talent myself, and my ministers are inferior to me, so the state of Chu is truly in danger.' You are joyful about what King Zhuang of Chu was worried about. I am deeply concerned." Marquis Wu thus felt embarrassed.

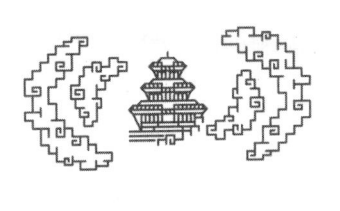

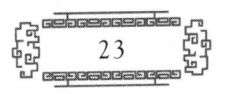

CHAPTER II.

KNOWING THE ENEMY

WUZI

1

Marquis Wu said to Wu Qi: "Now the state of Qin is threatening my west, Chu is surrounding my south, Zhao is facing my north, Qi is closing in on my east, Yan is blocking my back, Han is in front of me, and the armies of the six states are encircling us.

2

This unfavourable condition is worrying. What should I do?"

3

Wu Qi replied: "The most crucial way to secure the state is to be prepared first.

4

Now that you are on guard, you are far away from the scourge.

KNOWING THE ENEMY

5

Allow me to analyse the situation of the six states' military formations: Qi's formation is huge but not strong; Qin's formation is scattered but can fight separately; Chu's formation is strict but not sustainable; Yan's formation is long on defence but short on maneuver; Han and Zhao's formations are neat but not effective.

6

The Qi people are strong by nature and the state is rich.

7

But its ruler and ministers are arrogant and extravagant; they neglect the interests of their people; the decrees are lax and salaries unevenly distributed; the hearts and minds of their people are not united; the deployment of their troops is heavy in the front and light in the back, so the formation is huge but not strong.

WUZI

8

The way to fight against them is to divide our troops into three parts; two launch side attacks on their left and right flanks, and one takes advantage of the situation to attack from the front to disrupt their formation.

9

The Qin people are tough and its terrain is dangerous; its government is strict; the rewards and punishments are clear; their soldiers are ambitious and have a strong fighting spirit, so they can fight separately in a scattered formation.

10

The way to fight against them is to entice them with profit.

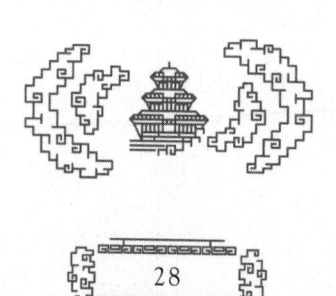

KNOWING THE ENEMY

11

When their soldiers are out of the grasp of its general due to the competition for profit, then we can strike their scattered troops amid the confusion, and set up ambush troops to boost the opportunity to win; then its general can be captured as well.

12

The Chu people are soft and weak by nature; their territory is vast; their government is dysfunctional and their people are weary.

13

Therefore, although their formation is strict and neat, it cannot last.

14

The way to fight against them is to attack its garrison to first destroy their morale, then to attack suddenly and retreat suddenly to wear them down instead of confronting them.

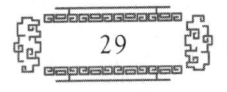

WUZI

15

Their army can be defeated as a result.

16

The Yan people are honest and cautious in their actions; their men are righteous and fraudulence and espionage are rarely seen there.

17

They are good at defending but not at manoeuvring.

18

The way to fight against them is to suppress their force as soon as our troops meet.

KNOWING THE ENEMY

19

Retreat immediately after attack and try to disrupt their back, feeding suspicion among their general and soldiers.

20

Then deploy our chariots and horses on their retreat route for an ambush, and their generals can be captured by us.

21

Han and Zhao are the states of the Central China; their people are docile and their government is peaceful.

22

The people there are tired of crippling scourges; they have been in war for a long time, and they despise their generals and are dissatisfied with the way they are treated.

WUZI

23

Their soldiers are not loyal, either.

24

Although their formation is neat, it is not feasible.

25

The way to fight against them is to approach with a strong formation, block them as they attack, and chase them as they retreat to wear them down. This is the general situation of the six states.

26

In that case, there must be tremendous warriors in the army, whose strength can easily lift a tripod, and who can move lightly and quickly enough to chase a war horse.

KNOWING THE ENEMY

27

There must be such capable men in order to capture the enemy flag and kill the enemy general, such talents must be selected, loved and assigned important positions; they are the essence of the army.

28

Anyone who is skilled at using various weapons, and strong, agile and determined to kill the enemy must be promoted to a higher rank, so that they can be used in battles to win.

29

Treat their parents and wives well, encourage them with reward, and warn them with punishment, so that they can become the backbone of a strengthened army for a lasting battle.

WUZI

30

If you can grasp these issues, you can defeat the enemy exponentially."

31

Marquis Wu said: "Very well!"

32

Wu Qi said: "There are eight cases of judging the enemy and engaging them without divination.

33

The first is that the enemy marches day and night in high winds and severe cold, cutting wood, crossing rivers and disregarding the hardships of the troops.

KNOWING THE ENEMY

34

Second, the enemy have a late start in the heat of summer without having rest on the way.

35

Their troops march rapidly and suffer hunger and thirst, only to rush to a distant land.

36

Third, the enemy troops have been out for a long time; their food is exhausted; the soldiers are angry; rumours repeatedly rise and the general cannot improve the situation.

37

Fourth, the enemy resources are depleted without enough firewood and grass for horses.

WUZI

38

Rainy weather persists and there is nowhere to acquire resources.

39

Fifth, the enemy troops are low in number and ill-adapted to local conditions.

40

Soldiers as well as horses fall sick without reinforcements coming to the rescue.

41

Sixth, their destination is distant and the day is getting dark.

KNOWING THE ENEMY

42

The enemy troops suffer fatigue and fear; they are sleepy and hungry and have to put away armour and weapons to rest.

43

Seventh, the enemy general has no authority and the morale is low.

44

The three armies repeatedly panic without any assistance.

45

Eighth, their deployment is not properly set; camping is not finished; and marching is only halfway through treacherous terrain such as mountains.

WUZI

46

When facing these situations, strike without any hesitation."

47

"There are six situations in which you should avoid fighting the enemy without divination.

48

First, a vast land with a large population and sufficient reserves.

49

Second, the seniors love their subordinates.

50

And rewards are distributed universally.

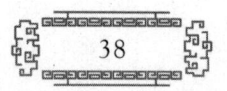

KNOWING THE ENEMY

51

Third, rewards and punishment are strictly implemented and actions are taken promptly.

52

Fourth, officials are given ranks based on their merits; only the wise and capable are appointed.

53

Fifth, the army is large, strong and well-equipped.

54

Sixth, neighbours and large states are ready to provide help and support.

WUZI

55

Whenever the enemy prove to be superior to you in these six conditions, avoid confrontation without hesitation.

56

Advance when the situation allows and retreat when difficulties loom large."

57

Marquis Wu asked: "I would like to know the enemy's internal situation by observing its external manifestations, and to know its true intentions from observing its actions so as to determine the result of victory or defeat.

58

Can you tell me the essentials of this?"

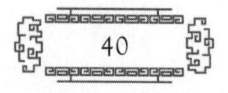

KNOWING THE ENEMY

59

Wu Qi replied: "If the enemy move in a scattered and careless manner and if their banners are disorganised and their men and horses look hesitant as they march forward, then strike ten of them with one blow.

60

That would suffice to cause panic among the enemy.

61

If the lords fail to meet up; if the rulers and ministers do not agree and their fortifications remain uncompleted; if bans are not enforced and the three armies are chaotic on the enemy's side, they are unable to advance and retreat.

62

In such a situation, deploy your troops in half size of their number and strike; you can win a hundred battles without a single loss."

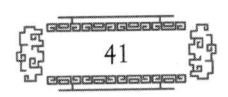

WUZI

63

Marquis Wu asked under what circumstances could his army strike the enemy.

64

Wu Qi replied: "To mobilise the army, we must find out the enemy's strengths and attack their weaknesses instead.

65

It is the time to strike when: the enemy are new to a place and have not yet decided on deployment; they have just finished meals and are not prepared; they are running around in panic; they are tired; they do not occupy favourable terrain; they suffer from unfavourable weather; their troops are in disorder; they take a long march without proper resting; they wade through water; they pass through treacherous roads; they frequently shift formations; their general is separated from the troops; their army is in a state of terror.

KNOWING THE ENEMY

66

Whenever these situations take place, first send the elite troops to charge forward and continue by deploying reinforcements; advance swiftly without hesitation."

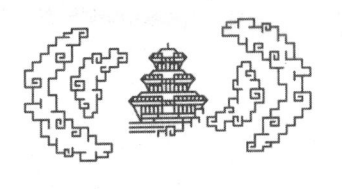

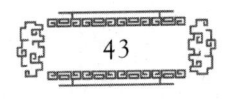

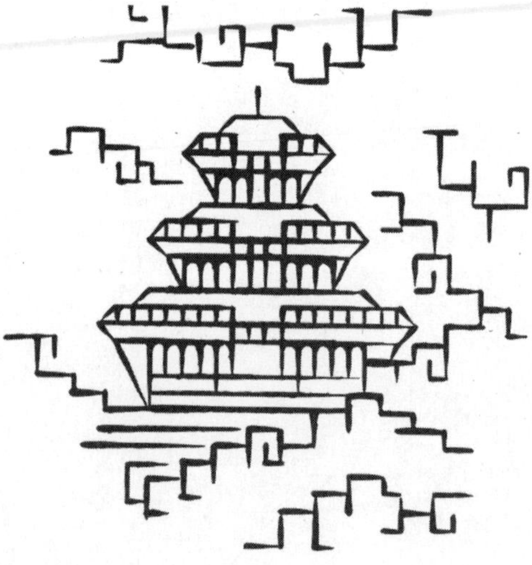

CHAPTER III.

ARMY MANAGEMENT

WUZI

1

Marquis Wu asked: "What is the primary strategy of the deployment of troops?"

2

Wu Qi replied: "First of all, we must bear in mind the ideas of 'four lightnesses', 'two heavinesses', and 'one trust'."

3

Marquis Wu: "Would you elaborate?"

4

Wu Qi: "The 'four lightnesses' refer to the fact that the terrain feels that the horses are light; the horses feel that the chariots are light; the chariots feel that the soldiers on it are light; and the soldiers feel that the burden of war is light.

ARMY MANAGEMENT

5

If you know the terrain and use it well, you will be able to ride your horses.

6

If the horses are kept in good condition, it is easy for them to drive chariots.

7

If the axles are frequently lubricated, the chariots are convenient for carrying men.

8

Sharp weapons and strong armour make it easier for men to fight.

WUZI

9

The 'two heavinesses' point to the approach of giving heavy reward to those fighting in close combat and heavy punishment for those in retreat.

10

The 'one trust' is to be trustworthy in managing reward and punishment.

11

If you can achieve these, you are bound to triumph."

12

Marquis Wu asked: "What does an army rely on to win battles?"

ARMY MANAGEMENT

13

Wu Qi replied: "A well-governed army can win battles."

14

Marquis Wu: "The size of troops doesn't matter?"

15

Wu Qi: "If the decree is not strict; if reward and punishment are not creditable; and if gong-beating does not stop soldiers and drum-beating does not motivate them to advance, then what is the use of having millions of military men?

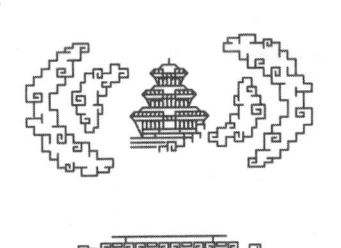

WUZI

16

If an army is to achieve good governance, it shall abide by the rituals and laws in peaceful time, be combative in wartime, be unstoppable when advancing, be unchasable when retreating and be restrained when advancing and retreating; it shall conform to the command when moving from side to side, maintain their respective formations even when they are separated and recover their ranks even when they are scattered.

17

The top and the bottom share weal and woe.

18

Then the army can be united without being separated, and can fight continuously without being exhausted.

19

They are unstoppable wherever they are marching.

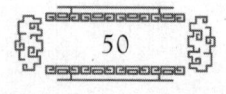

ARMY MANAGEMENT

20

This is what is called a 'father-and-son army' when all military men stand firm and united together."

21

Wu Qi said: "The general principle of deployment in battles is not to disrupt the rhythm of advancing and halting, not to delay food and drink supply, and not to exhaust the strength of men and horses.

22

These three factors are to keep the army in full strength to be able to perform the missions assigned by their superiors.

23

Such is the foundation of military governance.

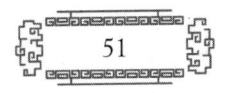

WUZI

24

If there is disorder in advancing and halting; if food and drink are not provided in a timely manner; and if men and horses are weary and unable to rest, the army will not fulfil the missions given by its superiors.

25

The orders of the superiors will not be carried out; the garrison will descend into chaos, and the battle will surely be lost."

26

Wu Qi said: "Where two armies fight, bloodshed and sacrifice are all but inevitable.

27

If you are committed to death, you are likely to survive; but if you only struggle to survive, you are likely to be destroyed.

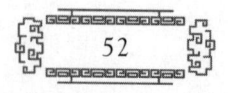

ARMY MANAGEMENT

28

Therefore, a general who is good at commanding a battle shall make sure that his troops act as if they are sitting in a leaky boat or lying under a burning house.

29

For in such an emergency, even a wise man has no time to plan carefully, and a brave man has no time to vent his anger; the immediate move is to swiftly make a decision and strike back.

30

Therefore, it is said that hesitation causes the greatest harm to the army; defeats mostly arise as a consequence of hesitation."

31

Wu Qi said: "In war, deaths are mainly due to a lack of strategies, and defeat, lack of warfare principles.

WUZI

32

Therefore, training is the top priority as the way to manage troops.

33

As one man learns the combat skills, he can teach ten other people.

34

These ten men can teach another one hundred people.

35

Theses one hundred men can teach another one thousand people.

36

These one thousand men can teach yet another ten thousand people.

ARMY MANAGEMENT

37

And ten thousand men can teach the whole three armies.

38

In warfare, set up formations in the vicinity of your own state to lure the enemy from afar; let your army rest well to meet the exhausted enemy soldiers; make sure your soldiers are strong with a full stomach to meet a hungry enemy army.

39

In formation, adapt your army to a variety of changes: from a round formation to a square one, from a sitting formation to a standing one, from advancing to halting, from a left formation to a right one, from a forward formation to a backward one, from a dispersion to an assembly and the vice versa.

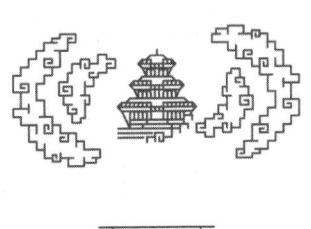

WUZI

40

Make sure your troops are well-trained for all kinds of formation changes before granting them weapons. These are the responsibilities of a general."

41

Wu Qi said: "To prepare soldiers for warfare: those who are short shall take spears; those who are tall shall use bows and arrows; those who are strong shall carry large banners; those who are brave shall operate golden drums; those who are weak shall serve as breeders and those who are wise shall be responsible for planning.

42

Soldiers from the same town and village shall be grouped together, and those who are in the same groups shall ensure mutual protection.

ARMY MANAGEMENT

43

Beat drums for five minutes to arrange weapons, ten minutes to practice formation, fifteen minutes to speed up eating, twenty minutes to get ready for battle and twenty-five minutes to assemble in formation.

44

Beat the drums in unison, then raise the flag to command the army to march."

45

Marquis Wu asked: "Is there a certain principle for marching and stationing?"

46

Wu Qi replied: "Do not camp at the 'heavenly stove' or station the troops at the 'dragon head'.

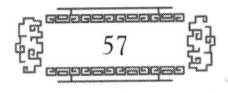

WUZI

47

'Heavenly stove' is the mouth of a deep valley; and 'dragon head' is the top of a high mountain.

48

In order to command the army, equip the left army with a flag emblazoned with a blue dragon, the right army with a white tiger flag, the front army with a vermilion bird flag and the back army with a turtle flag.

49

The middle army shall carry a waving flag to command the whole troops by occupying a high position.

50

Before the advent of battle, observe the direction of wind: charge forward in tailwind to take advantage of the momentum and bide your time in tailwind while maintaining a firm formation."

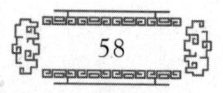

ARMY MANAGEMENT

51

Marquis Wu asked: "What is the method of taming military horses?"

52

Wu Qi replied: "The place of keeping military horses shall be comfortable; water and grass shall be properly fed to them, and strike a balance between their hunger and satiety.

53

Keep the stables warm in winter and cool in summer.

54

Trim and brush their manes on a regular basis.

55

Carefully clean their hooves and nails.

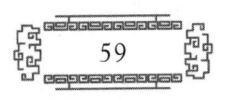

WUZI

56

Make sure they are adapted to various sounds and colours so that they are not prone to shocks.

57

Train them to run and chase in line with marching and stationing of the troops.

58

They are only tamed after the harmony between men and horses is achieved.

59

The horse-riding equipment such as saddles, bridles, snaffle bits and reins shall stay intact and solid.

ARMY MANAGEMENT

60

Horses are injured either at the end of their use or at the beginning of their use.

61

They are injured either due to excessive hunger or excessive food.

62

When the time is late and the journey is long, it is necessary to alternate between horse-riding and walking.

63

It is better for soldiers to be fatigued than for horses to be weary.

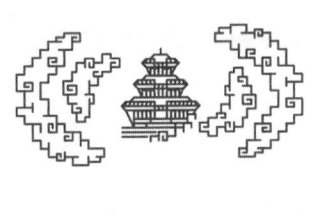

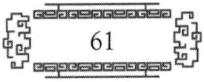

WUZI

64

Always keep the horses strong enough to prevent enemy attacks.

65

Those who master these will be invincible."

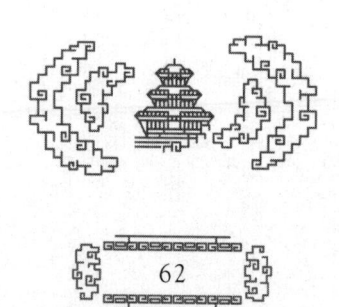

CHAPTER IV.

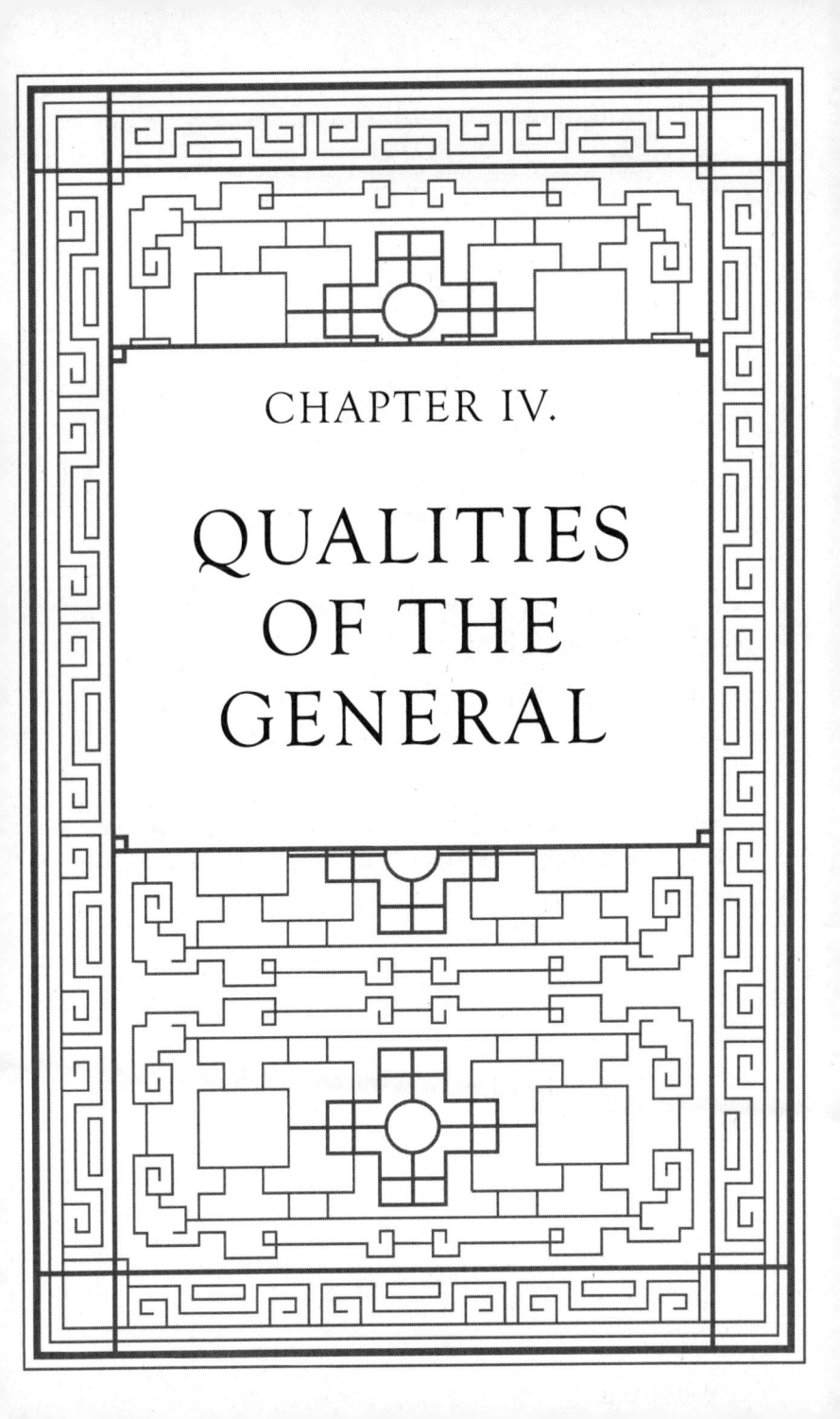

QUALITIES OF THE GENERAL

WUZI

1

Wu Qi said: "A person who has both civil and military skills can be a competent general.

2

Only those who can combine both rigidity and flexibility can command an army in battle.

3

The evaluation of a general is normally only associated with his bravery; but in fact, bravery is only one of several conditions that a general should have.

4

If one commands with bravery, he will certainly be rash to fight without considering the advantages and disadvantages.

QUALITIES OF THE GENERAL

5

In this case, he is not an eligible commander.

6

Therefore, there are five factors that a general should focus on: order, preparation, valour, caution and regulation.

7

Order is achieved when a large size of troops is governed in the same way as a small size of troops.

8

Preparation is achieved when the troops march in an alert manner as if they are facing the enemy.

WUZI

9

Valour is achieved when the general confronts the enemy without considering his personal death or life.

10

Caution is achieved when discretion comes first both upon victories and before battles.

11

Regulation is achieved when rules are simple and not cumbersome.

12

It is a principle that a general shall observe that he never shirks his duty and shall consider returning to his division only after he has defeated the enemy.

QUALITIES OF THE GENERAL

13

Therefore, from the day he heads for battle, a general shall make up his mind that he would rather die with honour than live with shame."

14

Wu Qi said: "There are four keys to commanding the army: to know the morale, to use terrain, to employ strategies, and to enrich strength.

15

To know the morale is to be well aware of the rise and fall of morale in the three armies with a million men; the responsibility lies in the general alone.

16

To use terrain is to take advantage of narrow and treacherous roads in key points on major mountains; in so doing, even ten men can safeguard against one thousand enemy soldiers.

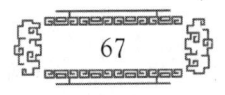

WUZI

17

To employ strategies is to send spies to sow discord in the enemy; send light-armed troops repeatedly to disrupt the enemy as a source of distraction, resulting in complaining and blaming among their rulers and ministers as well as the upper and lower ranks.

18

To enrich strength is to solidify wheel pins of chariots, improve the sculls and oars of boats, train the soldiers to practice various battle formations and prepare the horses for racing.

19

Only when one masters these four can he be qualified for a general.

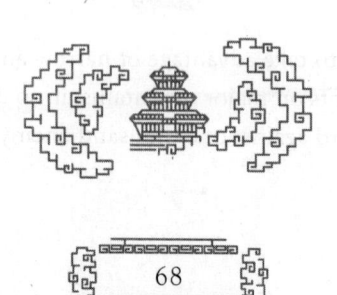

QUALITIES OF THE GENERAL

20

Moreover, his prestige, character, benevolence and bravery must be sufficient to lead the whole army, appease the soldiers, deter the enemy and resolve doubts.

21

He must be able to issue orders that his men will not dare to disobey; wherever he goes, the enemy will not dare to resist.

22

If you have such a general, your state will stand strong; but if you lose him, your state will perish.

23

This is what makes a good general."

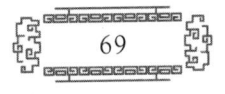

WUZI

24

Wu Qi said: "Drums and golden bells are meant to serve as auditory signals to command the army, while flags and banners are visual signals.

25

Prohibition and punishment are the law and discipline used to restrain the whole army.

26

Sounds shall not be unclear for the soldiers to hear; colours shall not be ambiguous for them to see; punishment shall not be relaxed for them to know by heart.

27

If these three principles are not implemented, a state is doomed to be defeated by its enemy.

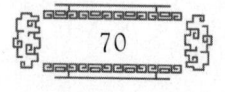

QUALITIES OF THE GENERAL

28

Therefore, there is no order issued by the general that the troops shall not follow.

29

There is no place to which the general directs and the troops shall not go forward and willingly risk their lives."

30

Wu Qi said: "In warfare, the top priority is to first find out who the enemy general is and to know him.

31

Employ flexible strategies in correspondence with the enemy's situations, then you will succeed without much effort.

WUZI

32

If the enemy general is stupid and gullible, use deception to lure him.

33

If the enemy general is greedy with poor integrity, bribe him.

34

If the enemy general changes his plans rashly without farsightedness, wear him down.

35

If the enemy upper ranks are rich and arrogant and its lower ranks poor and resentful, sow discord.

QUALITIES OF THE GENERAL

36

If the enemy troops are lost and indecisive in moving and retreating, scare them away.

37

If a soldier from the enemy troops despises his general and is eager to return home, block off the easy routes and lay ambush on the trickier roads.

38

If the enemy has an easy way in and a difficult way out, lure them in before destroying them all.

39

If the enemy has a difficult way in but an easy way out, approach them and attack.

WUZI

40

If the enemy camp in a low-lying and wet place where waterways are inaccessible and heavy rains are continuous, flood them with water and drown them.

41

If the enemy camp in a swamp with grass, trees and gusts of wind, destroy them by fire attack.

42

If the enemy camp for a long time without marching forward, wait for them to be lax and negligent before launching a sudden attack.

43

Marquis Wu asked: "When two armies face each other while we do not know the enemy general, what is to be done to find out?"

QUALITIES OF THE GENERAL

44

Wu Qi replied: "Send brave subordinate officers to lead light-armed troops for an attack.

45

Be sure to lose and retreat instead of trying to win. Observe the enemy when they come.

46

If the enemy advances and stops each time in an orderly way, and if they feign being unable to catch up and pretend not to see the easy gains, their general must be wise and tactful.

47

In this case, do not engage him.

WUZI

48

On the other hand, if the enemy is noisy; if their banners are in disarray; if their soldiers move wildly and weapons are scattered; and if they fear not catching up and not getting gains, their general is witless and he can be captured even when he leads a large size of troops."

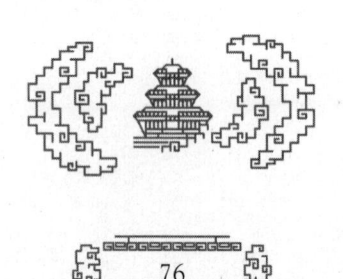

CHAPTER V.

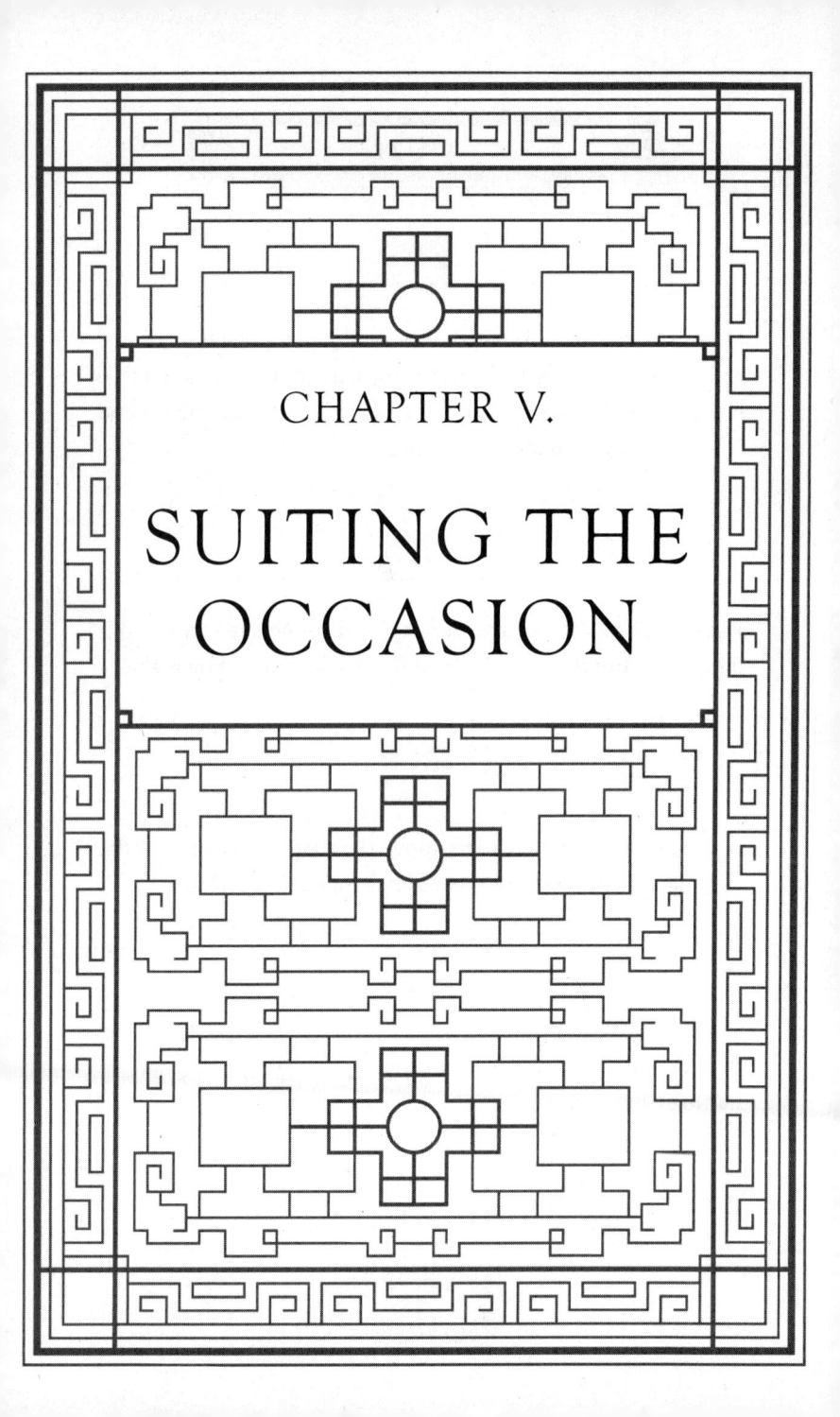

SUITING THE OCCASION

WUZI

1

Marquis Wu asked: "What should we do if we encounter an enemy unexpectedly while our troops are in disorder and out of line but the chariots are solid, the horses are tamed, the general is brave, and the soldiers are strong?"

2

Wu Qi replied: "In warfare, use flags and banners to command by day, and to use gongs, drums and flutes to command by night.

3

If the command is to the left, move the troops to the left; if the command is to the right, move the troops to the right.

4

Beat the drums to signal advancing and the gongs to signal halting.

SUITING THE OCCASION

5

The first time the flute is blown, march forward; the second time the flute is blown, assemble the men.

6

Those who fail to obey the command shall be killed.

7

When the three armies adhere to the authority of the command and the soldiers duly obey the orders, there will be no strong enemy that cannot be defeated, and no formation that cannot be broken down."

8

Marquis Wu asked: "What should we do if the enemy outnumber us?"

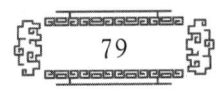

WUZI

9

Wu Qi replied: "Avoid fighting in open land; instead, intercept the enemy on dangerous terrain.

10

Therefore, it is best to use narrow roads to strike ten with one, dangerous terrain to strike one hundred with ten, and blocked areas to strike ten thousand with one thousand.

11

If you use a small size of troops, launch a sudden attack in narrow terrain while drumming aloud.

12

As a result, the enemy will be subjected to panic and commotion despite their larger size.

SUITING THE OCCASION

13

Therefore, large troops shall be deployed in open land, while small troops shall take advantage of rough terrain."

14

Marquis Wu asked: "The enemy is strong in size, well-trained and brave; they have tall mountains behind, advantageous location in front, mountains to the right and water to the left; they boast deep trenches, high barriers and strong crossbows as defence.

15

They retreat as firmly as a mountain and march forward as fast as the wind and rain; their food reserve is also abundant.

16

A protracted battle with them is daunting. What should we do?"

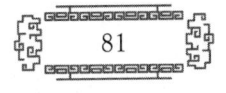

WUZI

17

Wu Qi replied: "What a complicated question! The strength of the troops alone is far from enough; a wise use of strategy is the key to win.

18

If we can prepare ten chariots, cavalry of ten thousand soldiers as well as infantry, divide them into five units and send each in a different direction.

19

With five units of soldiers marching from five different directions, this move will cause confusion among the enemy, who cannot tell where the strike will take place.

20

If the enemy is solidly on the defensive by reinforcements, an envoy shall be sent immediately to find out their intentions.

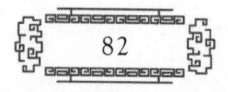

SUITING THE OCCASION

21

If they heed our advice and withdraw their troops, we shall follow suit.

22

However, they may also refuse and decide to kill the envoy and burn the goodwill letters.

23

In this case, strike from five directions; but do not pursue them if the battle is won and withdraw swiftly if the battle is lost.

24

If you are to entrap the enemy by feigning defeat, move steadily with one unit of soldiers and fight violently; meanwhile, for the other four units of soldiers: one is to pin down the enemy in the front; one is to to cut off their route of retreat; and the other two are to move secretively and attack their stronghold from the left and right sides.

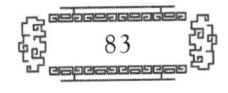

WUZI

25

The five units of soldiers combined contribute to a favourable condition for us.

26

This is the way to combat strong enemy."

27

Marquis Wu asked: "The enemy is approaching and forcing us to engage, but there is no way out, causing fear in our army. What should be done?"

28

Wu Qi replied: "The solution to this problem is: if the enemy is outnumbered by us, we shall divide our troops to surround them.

SUITING THE OCCASION

29

If the opposite is the case, we shall bring our forces together to strike consistently; in so doing, the enemy will be subdued despite their large size."

30

Marquis Wu asked: "If we encounter the enemy between a stream and a valley with treacherous terrain on both sides and we are outnumbered by them, what should be done?"

31

Wu Qi replied: "Faced with unfavourable terrain such as hills, forests, valleys, deep mountains, and large swamps, pass quickly without delay.

32

If we unexpectedly encounter the enemy in a high mountain and deep valley, beat the drums and shout first before taking advantage of the situation to disrupt the enemy.

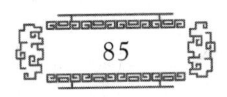

WUZI

33

Then deploy archers to the front on guard while reflecting on counter strategies.

34

Observe whether the enemy's formation is in disarray.

35

When chaos arises, launch an attack with all our might without hesitation."

36

Marquis Wu asked: "The land is narrow with high mountains on either side. What should be done upon an unforeseen encounter with the enemy when we dare not attack but cannot retreat?"

SUITING THE OCCASION

37

Wu Qi replied: "This is the situation when valley warfare takes place.

38

In this case, it is not the large size of troops that matters.

39

The best and brightest soldiers shall be selected to confront the enemy; send agile and fast soldiers with sharp weapons as the vanguard.

40

Scatter the chariots and horses around for an ambush at a distance of several miles from the vanguard, so as not to reveal the true strength.

WUZI

41

As a result, the enemy will definitely hold their position instead of venturing for advance or retreat.

42

At this time, one unit of soldiers shall be sent out of the mountain with flags and banners to further confuse and disturb the enemy, giving rise to their fear.

43

Then disrupt the enemy with chariots and horses to the point that they cannot rest.

44

This is the method of warfare in valley."

SUITING THE OCCASION

45

Marquis Wu asked: "Faced with the enemy in a place where floods converge and water inundates the wheels and submerges the handles of chariots, our chariots and horses are in danger of being engulfed. However, no boats are at disposal while we are stuck in limbo between advance and retreat. What can be done?"

46

Wu Qi replied: "This is the situation when water warfare takes place.

47

Chariots and horses are of no use, so leave them on the shore temporarily.

WUZI

48

Climb up high and observe the four directions to grasp the water situation, including the width and depth of the floods in order to win by surprise.

49

If the enemy comes through the water, strike them when they are halfway across."

50

Marquis Wu asked: "It's been raining relentlessly and difficult to move chariots and horses forward; we are besieged by the enemy and the whole army is in fear. What can be done?"

51

Wu Qi replied: "Whenever we fight with chariots, stop when it is rainy and muddy, and move on when the ground is dry and clear.

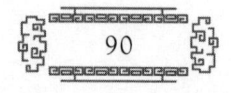

SUITING THE OCCASION

52

Take higher ground and avoid lower areas; move chariots in a swift manner; always take advantage of roads no matter we advance or halt.

53

If enemy chariots move on muddy land, do follow their tracks."

54

Marquis Wu asked: "What should be done when a violent enemy strikes by plundering crops and stealing cattle and sheep?"

55

Wu Qi replied: "When a violent enemy attacks, this should be considered.

WUZI

56

Respond by defence instead of counterattack.

57

When the enemy withdraw in the evening, their load must be heavy and their mind fearful; they seek to retreat quickly and there must be stragglers.

58

Seize this opportunity to chase and destroy them."

59

Wu Qi said: "The general principle of siege: once the enemy's city or fief is broken into, station troops in its governmental offices and keep their officials under control while taking over their equipment and resources.

SUITING THE OCCASION

60

Our army is not allowed to cut down trees, destroy houses, take crops, slaughter livestock, or burn warehouses so as to show that they are not brutes to local people.

61

If there are people who offer to surrender, acknowledge and pacify them."

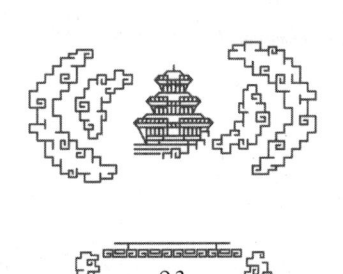

CHAPTER VI.

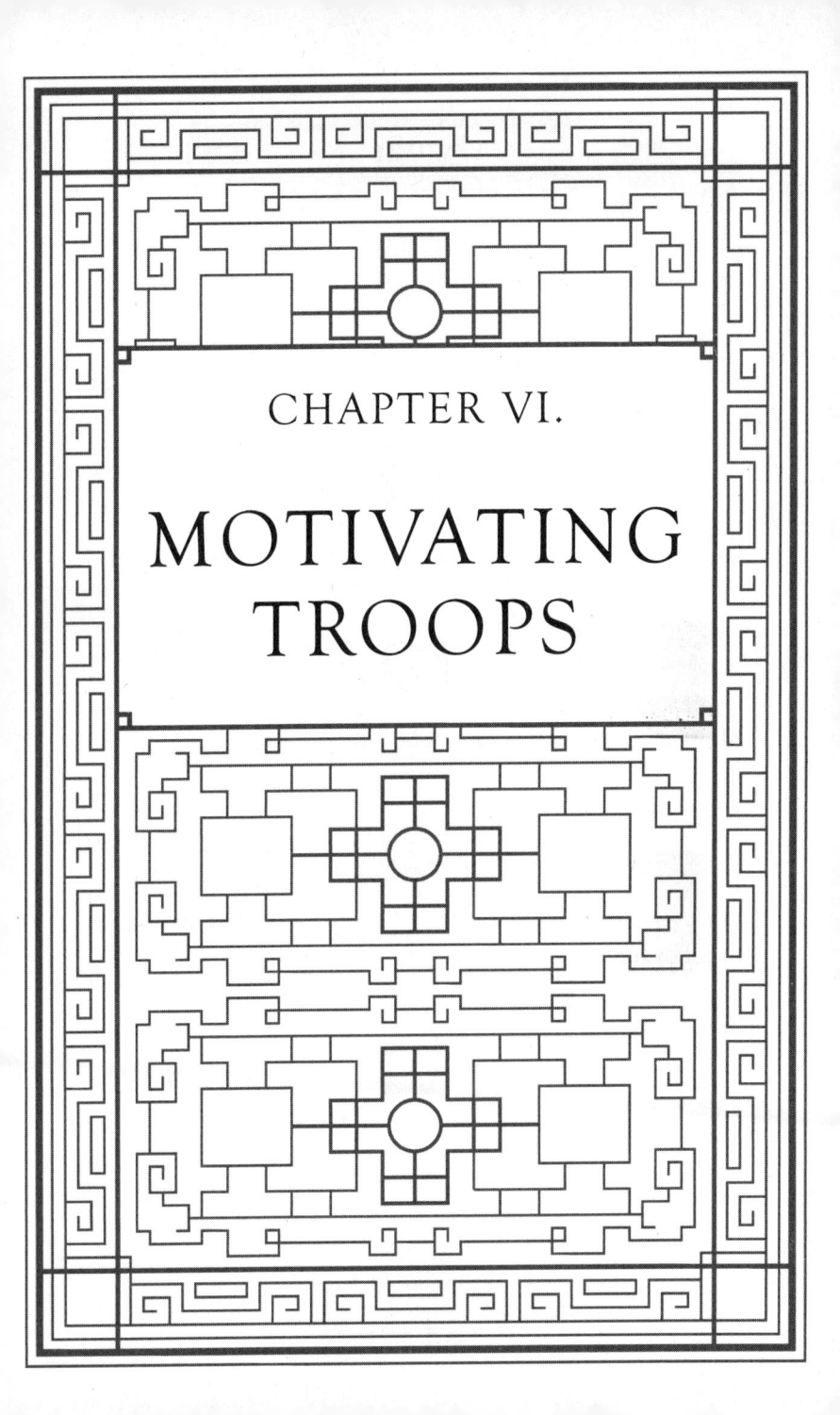

MOTIVATING TROOPS

WUZI

1

Marquis Wu asked: "Is a strict management of reward and punishment sufficient to win a battle?"

2

Wu Qi replied: "I cannot give an exhaustive account of this matter.

3

Although it is critical, it cannot be fully relied upon.

4

What you need are people who willingly take orders for war, go to battle and die when they fight.

5

These are the three factors that a monarch should rely on."

MOTIVATING TROOPS

6

Marquis Wu: "How can I achieve that?"

7

Wu Qi: "Select accomplished men and throw a lavish banquet to entertain them, which also inspires those who are not accomplished yet."

8

Marquis Wu thus hosted a banquet at the ancestral temple and invited scholar-officials and had them seated in three rows.

9

Those who had achieved the highest merit sat in the front row with the finest wine, precious tableware, and meals containing pork, beef and goat.

WUZI

10

Those with second-class merit sat in the middle row, with lesser meals and cutlery.

11

Those without merit sat in the back row with only meals and no expensive tableware.

12

As the banquet closed, the parents and wives of the accomplished officers were rewarded outside the temple gate, also in different rows according to their merits.

13

As for the families of the sacrificed soldiers, envoys were sent to meet the parents of the fallen soldiers to offer condolences and rewards on a yearly basis, so as to show that the deceased were well remembered.

MOTIVATING TROOPS

14

After three years of this practice, the Qin army descended on the border of Wei at the West River.

15

As the Wei soldiers were informed, tens of thousands of them put on armour and fought valiantly against the enemy without waiting for orders from officials.

16

Marquis Wu then summoned Wu Qi and told him: "The methods you taught me before are now bearing fruit."

17

Wu Qi replied: "I have heard that men have shortcomings and strengths; morale also rises and falls.

WUZI

18

You might as well dispatch fifty thousand unaccomplished men, who are led by me to fight against the Qin army.

19

If they lose the battle, we will be ridiculed by the other states, resulting in our diminishing authority.

20

Think about this: there is a thief who has committed a capital crime and is on the run in the wilderness.

21

In this case, when one thousand men are sent to go after him, all of them will be highly wary.

MOTIVATING TROOPS

22

Why is that? Because they are afraid that the thief will suddenly strike and cause harm.

23

So, one man's action out of desperation is enough to make one thousand men quiver.

24

Now all my fifty thousand men can be likened to that thief; so if I lead them to confront the enemy, the enemy is doomed to be crushed."

25

Marquis Wu took Wu Qi's advice and sent an additional five hundred chariots with three thousand war horses.

WUZI

26

They succeeded in defeating the five hundred thousand men of the Qin army.

27

This is what motivating troops can achieve.

28

On the day before the battle, Wu Qi addressed his three armies: "All the officials and soldiers shall obey the orders to fight. To the chariot soldiers, cavalry and infantry: if the chariot soldiers cannot capture the enemy's chariot soldiers, and the cavalry cannot capture the enemy's cavalry and the infantry cannot capture the enemy's infantry, you will not be considered as accomplished even if you defeat them."

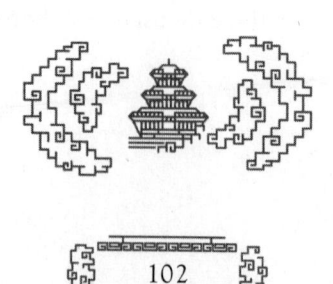

MOTIVATING TROOPS

29

Therefore, on the day of the battle, Wu Qi merely sent a limited number of orders while achieving victories and inspiring awe.

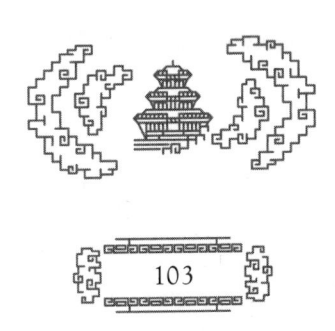